CU00684066

COVER ILLUSTRATIONS

Front The first page of the 'Laws of Æthelberht' – 'not only the earliest English document but also by far the earliest text of any kind in something like the language we use' (*page 9*). The stain on this and other pages of the *Textus Roffensis* resulted from the brief submersion of the book in 1712 when the barge returning it from London to Rochester sank in the Medway.

Back The Kingston Brooch (*Liverpool Museum*), found in a female barrow burial on Kingston Down, near Canterbury, by Brian Faussett in 1771. The Canterbury Pendant (*Museum of Canterbury*), found in 1982 by Jonathan Rady, of the Canterbury Archaeological Trust, while monitoring the digging of foundation trenches for a building in London Road, Canterbury. It lay in two pieces in a disturbed Anglo-Saxon inhumation burial. Similar in conception and technique, these two finds reveal how Anglo-Saxon jewellers adapted their repertoire to meet new, Christian needs. Both pieces show – and indeed were designed to project – the wealth of high-status individuals in Æthelberht's Kent.

Patrick Wormald 1947 - 2004

Formerly Fellow of All Souls College, Oxford,
Lecturer in Mediaeval History, University of Glasgow and
Student of Christ Church, Oxford

Author of *The Making of English Law*

From his obituary in The Times of 6 October 2004
'He was a pioneer of the new British history focused
on the multilingual and multicultural development of
these islands…In October 2003 Wormald gave a public
lecture at Canterbury …on Ethelbert's code of law, too
difficult a subject (one might have thought) for a lecture
to the public of Canterbury and Kent, proud as they might
be of their special heritage. But he was able to demonstrate
how exciting all this was: Kent possessed the first English
law code and the first writing in the English language….'

Originally entitled **King Æthelberht of the Kent-people
and the First English Code of Law,** this lecture (again
to quote *The Times*) 'encapsulated all his main ideas'. Its
argument culminates in an expression of heartfelt support
(*page 19*) for the idea of erecting statues of Æthelberht and
his Frankish queen.

The First Code
of English Law

PATRICK WORMALD

THE CANTERBURY COMMEMORATION SOCIETY

First published 2005

by the Canterbury Commemoration Society
with support from the Selden Society
and Furley Page Solicitors, Canterbury

Copyright © the Estate of Patrick Wormald 2005

ISBN0-9551196-0-X
978-0-9551196-0-6

Printed by Mickle Print, Canterbury

Contents

Illustrations: four pages between pages 8 and 9

1   Introducing King Æthelberht and his Laws

The history of England began in Kent fourteen hundred and seven years ago. The history of English law began within the next two decades. The arrival in 597 of Pope Gregory's mission introduced the pagan peoples of Kent and nearby kingdoms not only to Christianity but also, and therefore, to written records, the stock-in-trade of historians as opposed to prehistorians. The major source for this turning-point in the island's story is Gregory's own letters, followed up within a century and a half by Bede's immortal *Ecclesiastical History*.   The mission and letters were directed at King Æthelberht of the people of Kent (in their own language, *Cantwara*).   Before he died in 616 or 618, he equipped his kingdom with a codified statement of some of their law.   This was the first surviving text of any type written by as well as for Englishmen.   Later in the century, at about the same date as the first extant saints' lives and charters (title-deeds), there were two more codes of Kentish law, those of King Hlothere and Eadric (679-86) and of Wihtræd (695), and one issued by King Ine of Wessex (688-92).   After a gap of two centuries, the continuous story of English written law resumed under King Alfred (893-99), interrupted only for a space of forty years before the Norman Conquest and then for half a century before the great series of King Henry II's 'assizes' began in 1166.   Its distinctive legal system is one of the salient features of 'Englishness'.   That feature is first detectable in King Æthelberht's laws.

The code survives in just one copy, made in the early 1120s, so more than half a millennium after it was issued.   This poses in acute form the question whether our text can be anything like the one issued by Æthelberht and his councillors.   But there are two reasons to believe that it is.   The first is the nature of the manuscript itself, the famous *Textus Roffensis*, Rochester's Book, which still belongs to the Dean and Chapter.   This is more than an assemblage of any legal material coming under the author's eye.   It is almost all the work of one scribe, who also wrote other Rochester books.   There are grounds for thinking him a trusted servant of Bishop Ernulf of Rochester (1114-24). Ernulf himself was a friend or acquaintance of Bishop Ivo of Chartres (d. 1116), the greatest lawyer of the age. He would have learned from Ivo the analytical approach to contradictions in ancient legal texts which put a premium on having accurate and preferably dated copies. We can see that *Textus Roffensis* was put together from a variety of sources, sometimes updating the text as first copied. For example, the last item in Part I is a list of Popes, patriarchs and English bishops and kings, known to have been copied from one compiled at Canterbury, then brought up to date by Rochester's scribe. The maker of Rochester's book thus put a lot of effort into faithfully reproducing his texts.

The other reason is the code's language, whose character is as far as possible reflected in the following translation. It is highly archaic. More is said about this in 3. *Explanatory Comment*, but we can note for now that the meaning of *rithamscyld*; (cl. '32') is so entirely unknown that scholars differ as to whether it is about sexual behaviour or property boundaries. The syntax, especially of the 'personal injury' section [V] has the extreme simplicity thought typical of law formulated and transmitted only by memory and word of mouth; which is of course how law would have to have been recorded over the long ages before Christianity brought literacy to English-speaking peoples.

2. The Laws of King Æthelberht and the Kent people (*Cantwara*)

This translation – my own, though closely following Oliver's (see 5. Further Reading) is as consistently faithful to the wording of the original Kentish as I can make it without total sacrifice of modern grammar or sense. Its elliptical and repetitive style is one of the code's most important features, and a sign that it had previously been preserved orally. The original wording is given, where useful or revealing, in italics and round brackets; insertions by me or previous editors are in square brackets. Note, therefore, that there were no clause numbers in the original manuscript: chapter divisions are editorial, though Oliver's (in bold, and the ones followed in the Comment below) do follow the punctuation of the manuscript (italic numbers are those of Attenborough's long-established edition). Divisions marked by capital Roman numerals and square brackets are mine, meant to highlight the code's overall structure.

[I COMPENSATION OF CHURCH GOODS, ACCORDING TO CLERICAL RANK]

— [1]   God's goods (*feoh*) and the church's with payment twelvefold (*XII gylde*)

— [2]   Bishop's goods with payment x 11

— [3]   Priest's goods with payment x 9

— [4]   Deacon's goods with payment x 6

— [5]   Cleric's goods with payment x 3

— [6]   Church peace (*frið*) with payment x 2

— [7]   Assembly (*mæthl*) peace with payment x 2

[II COMPENSATION FOR KING'S POSSESSIONS AND DEPENDANTS]

— [*2* 8]   If the king summons his persons (*leode*) to him, and someone does harm to them there, with compensation x 2 (*II bote*) and fifty shillings to the king

— [*3* 9]   If the king is drinking at someone's home, and someone commit treachery (*lyswæs*) there, he is to compensate doubly (*twibote gebete*)

— [*4* 10] If a freeman (*frigman*) steal from the king, he is to pay up (*forgylde*) with payment x 9 (*IX gylde forgylde*)

— [*5* 11] If someone kill someone at a king's estate (*tune*), he is to compensate 50 shillings

— [*6* 12] If someone kills a freeman, 50 shillings to the king as lord-gift (*to drihtinbeage*)

— [*7* 13] If one kills the king's officer, smith or messenger, he is to pay up the person-payment (*leodgelde forgelde*)

— [*8* 14] The king's protection (*mundbyrd*), 50 shillings

— [*9* **15**]   If a freeman steal from a free, he is to compensate x 3 (*III gebete*), and the king is to possess the fine for that (*þæt wite*) or all the possessions (*æhtan*)

— [*10* **16**]   If someone lies with a king's maiden, he is to compensate 50 shillings

— [*11* **16:1**] If she be a grinding slave, he is to compensate 25 shillings

— [**16:2**]   The third [sc. rank?], 12 shillings

— [*12* **17**]   The king's feeding (*fedesl*), one is to pay up 20 shillings

[III COMPENSATION FOR EARL'S POSSESSIONS OR DEPENDANTS]

— [*13* **18**]   If someone kills someone at the earl's estate, he is to compensate 12 shillings

— [*14* **19**]   If someone lies with an earl's cupbearer (*birele*), he is to compensate 12 shillings

[IVa COMPENSATION FOR *CEORL*'S POSSESSIONS AND DEPENDANTS]

— [*15* **20**]   *Ceorl*'s protection, 6 shillings

— [*16* **21**]   If someone lies with a *ceorl*'s cupbearer, he is to compensate with 6 shillings

— [**21:1**]   For the second slave, 50 *scætta* [2 ½ sh.]

— [**21:2**]   For the third, 30 *scætta* [1 ½ sh.]

— [*17* **22**]   If someone breaks as first entrant into someone's estate (*tun*), he is to compensate with 6 shillings

— [**22:1**]   He who breaks second, 3 shillings

— [**22:2**]   Each man afterward, a shilling

— [*18* **23**]   If someone supply someone with weapons when conflict happens, and one does not do any harm, he is to compensate with 6 shillings

— [*19* **23:1**] If highway robbery (*wegreaf*) be done, he is to compensate with 6 shillings

— [*20* **23:2**] If someone kills that man, he is to compensate with 20 shillings

— [*21* **24**] If someone kills someone, he is to compensate with an average person-payment (*medume leodgeld*), 100 shillings

— [*22* **24:1**] If someone kills someone, at the open grave he is to pay up 20 shillings, and to pay off the whole person in 40 nights

— [*23* **24:2**] If the killer leaves the country, the kinsmen are to pay half the person

— [*24* **25**] If someone binds a free man, he is to compensate 20 shillings

— [*25* **26**] If someone kills a *ceorl*'s loaf-eater (*hlafæta*), he is to compensate with 6 shillings

[V COMPENSATION FOR SEMI-FREE (*læt*)]

— [*26* **27**] If he kills a *læt*, for the top-rank (*selestan*), he is to pay up to 80 shillings

— [**27:1**] If he kills the second [grade], he is to pay up with 60 shillings

— [**27:2**] For the third, he is to pay up with 40 shillings

[IVb CEORL'S POSSESSIONS AND DEPENDANTS (*continued ?*)]

— [*27* **28**] If a freeman does enclosure-breach (*edorbrecthe*), he is to compensate with 6 shillings

— [*28* **28:1**] If someone takes goods therein, the man is to compensate with payment x 3

— [*29* **29**] If a freeman gets into an enclosure, he is to compensate with 4 shillings

—[*30* **30**] If someone kill a man, he is to pay with his own money (*scætte*) or unimpeachable goods (*unfacne feo*), whichever

— [*31* **31**] If a freeman lies with a free man's wife, he is to buy [?her] with his man-payment (*wergilde*), and obtain another wife with his own money and bring [her] to him at home

— [*32* **32**] If someone severs a legitimate marriage-liability [?!] (*rihtamscyld þurh stinð*), he is to pay for it with its value

[VI PERSONAL INJURIES]

—[*33* **33**] If hair-seizure takes place (*geweorð*), 50 *scætta* [2 ½ sh.] as compensation

— [*34* **34**] If exposure of bone takes place, one is to compensate with 4 shillings

— [*36* **36**] If the outer membrane becomes broken (*gebrocen weorþeð*), one is to compensate with 10 shillings

— [*37* **36:1**] If both be, one is to compensate with 20 shillings

— [*38* **37**] If a shoulder becomes lamed, one is to compensate with 30 shillings

— [*39* **38**] If either ear hears nothing, one is to compensate with 12 shillings

— [*40* **39**] If an ear becomes struck off, one is to compensate with 12 shillings

— [*41* **40**] If an ear becomes pierced, one is to compensate with 3 shillings

— [*42* **41**] If an ear becomes gashed, one is to compensate with 6 shillings

— [*43* **42**] If an eye becomes put out, one is to compensate with 50 shillings

— [*44* **43**] If a mouth or eye becomes damaged, one is to compensate with 12 shillings

— [*45* **44**] If a nose becomes pierced, one is to compensate with 9 shillings

— [*46* **44:1**] If it be on the cheek, one is to compensate with 3 shillings

— [*47* **44:2**] If both be pierced, one is to compensate with 6 shillings

— [*48* **45**] If a nose becomes gashed otherwise, one is to compensate with 6 shillings

— [*49* **46**] If a throat [?] becomes pierced, one is to compensate with 6 shillings

— [*50* **47**] He who smashes a chinbone is to pay up with 20 shillings

— [*51* **48**] For the four front teeth, for each 6 shillings

— [**48:1**] The tooth that comes next, 4 shillings

— [48:2]   That which comes next after that, 3 shillings

— [48:3]   And then each thereafter, a shilling

— [*52* 49]   If speech becomes damaged, 12 shillings

— [*52:1* 50]   If a collar-bone becomes broken, one is to compensate with 6 shillings

— [*53* 51]   He who transfixes an arm is to compensate with 6 shillings

— [*53:1* 52]   If the arm becomes broken, one is to compensate with 6 shillings

— [*54* 53]   If one strikes off a thumb, 20 shillings

— [*54:1* 54]   If a thumb-nail comes off, one is to compensate with 3 shillings

— [*54:2* 55]   If someone strikes off a shooting-finger, he is to compensate with 9 shillings

— [*54:3* 56]   If someone strikes off a middle-finger, he is to compensate with 4 shillings

— [*54:4* 57]   If someone strikes off a gold-finger, he is to compensate with 6 shillings

— [*54:5* 58]   If someone strikes off the little finger, he is to compensate with 11 shillings

— [*55* 59]   For each of the nails, a shilling

— [*56* 60]   For the slightest disfigurement, 3 shillings

— [60:1]   And for the greater, 6 shillings

— [*57* 61]   If someone strikes another on the nose with a fist, 3 shillings

— [*58* 61:1]   If it be a blow, a shilling

— [*58:1* 61:2]   If he receives a blow from a raised hand, one is to pay up a shilling

— [*59* 61:3]   If the blow be black outside clothing [leave a visible bruise], one is to compensate 30 *scætta* [1½ sh.]

— [*60* 61:4]   If it be within clothing, one is to compensate 20 *scætta* [1 sh.] for each

— [*61* 62]   If the stomach becomes wounded, one is to compensate with 12 shillings

— [*61:1* **62:1**] If it becomes transfixed, one is to compensate with 20 shillings

— [*62* **63**] If someone becomes cured [needs curing], one is to compensate with 30 shillings

— [*63* **63:1**] If someone be grievously wounded, one is to compensate with 30 shillings

— [*64* **64**] If someone disables a genital member (*gekyndelice lim*), one is to pay him off with three person-payments (*þrym leudgeldum*)

— [*64:1* **64:1**] If he transfixes, one is to compensate with 6 shillings

— [*64* **64:2**] If someone pierces, one is to compensate with 6 shillings

— [*65* **65**] If a thigh becomes broken, one is to compensate with 12 shillings

— [*65:1* **65:1**] If he becomes lame, then friends must settle

— [*66* **66**] If a rib becomes broken, one is to compensate with 3 shillings

— [*67* **67**] If someone transfixes a thigh, for each thrust 6 shillings

— [*67:1* **67:1**] If more than an inch, a shilling

— [**67:2**] For two inches, two

— [**67:3**] More than three, 3 shillings

— [*68* **68**] If a scar results, one is to compensate 3 shillings

— [*69* **69**] If a foot comes off (*of weorðeþ*), one is to pay up with 50 shillings

— [*70* **70**] If the big toe comes off, one is to pay up with 10 shillings

— [*71* **70:1**] For each of the other toes, one is to pay half as much as is declared for the fingers

— [*72* **71**] If the big toe-nail comes off, 30 *scætta* [1½ sh] as compensation

— [*72:1* **71:1**] For each of the others, one is to compensate 10 *scætta* [1½ sh.]

[VII WOMEN'S INJURIES AND POSSESSIONS]

— [*73* **72**] If a key-bearing freewoman commits any treachery, she is to compensate 30 shillings

The *Textus Roffensis* (Rochester Book) is a two-part compilation of English legal documents and the charters of Rochester Cathedral, made on the orders of Bishop Ernulf in 1122-24. The first section contains copies of three seventh-century Kentish law codes, which were seen as 'foundation documents' of the English state. It also includes the master copy of the coronation charter of Henry I (1100-35), the wording of which is echoed in Magna Carta (1215) and the American Declaration of Independence (1776). It consists of 234 leaves of parchment measuring 9 x 6 ½ inches (227 x 162 mm). The current binding dates from the eighteenth century. Formerly in Rochester Cathedral, it is now kept in the Medway Archive at Strood.

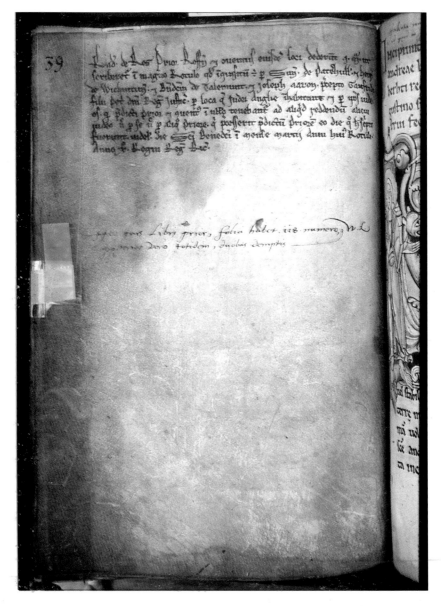

Folios 118v-119r of the *Textus Roffensis*. Above is the last page of Part One,
the collection of the ancient laws of England, and facing it is the first page of
Part Two, the catalogue of the possessions of Rochester Cathedral, beginning

with the illuminated capital 'R'. The two parts are complementary, the one asserting the continuity of the kingdom through its laws, and the other the rights and privileges of Rochester Cathedral under those laws.

Æthelberht's in-laws, the kings of the Franks, produced the 'Salic Law', the opening pages of which are shown in this eighth-century manuscript preserved in St Gallen, Switzerland (Stiftsbibliothek, MS 731, fol 234-5). Early in the seventh century, having a written code of law came to be seen in Western Europe as a mark of a people's civilization (*pages 16-17*). In contrast to the continental codes, however, Æthelberht's was in Old English, not Latin, and based on customary, not Roman, law (*page 17*). 'England's language and law are the most enduring marks of Englishness…The history of both begins with Æthelberht' (*page 19*).

— [*74* **73**] Compensation for a young girl (*mægþbot*) is to be as of a free man

— [*75* **74**] Protection of the foremost widow of noble birth (*betstan widuwan eorlcundre*) one is to compensate 50 shillings

— [*75:1* **74:1**] Of the second, 20 shillings

— [**74:2**] Of the third, 12 shillings

— [**74:3**] Of the fourth, 6 shillings

— [*76* **75**] If someone takes a widow not his own (*widuwan unagne*), the protection is to be with payment x 2

— [*77* **76**] If someone buys a girl for a price, it is a bargain (*geceapod sy*) if it is unimpeachable (*unfacne*)

— [*77:1* **76:1**] If it is impeachable, one is to take her home again, and someone is to give him his money (*scæt*)

— [*78* **76:2**] If she bears a living child, she is to possess half the money if her husband (*ceorl*) dies before

— [*79* **76:3**] If she wishes to live with the children, she is to possess half the money

— [*80* **76:4**] If she wishes to take a husband, as for one child

— [*81* **76:5**] If she does not bear a child, the father's kin are to possess the goods (*fioh*) and the morning-gift

— [*82* **77**] If someone takes a girl by force, 50 shillings to the possessor [i.e. protector], and one is afterwards to purchase his consent from the possessor

— [*83* **77:1**] If she be pledged (*beweddod*) to another man with money, one is to compensate 20 shillings

— [*84* **77:2**] If assault (*gængang*) takes place, 35 shillings and to the king 15 shillings

[VIII COMPENSATION FOR HANDYMEN (*esne*)]

— [*85* **78**] If someone lies with a handyman's wife in the husband's lifetime, he is to compensate x 2

— [*86* **79**] If a handyman kill another innocent, he is to pay off the whole value

— [*87* **80**]   If a handyman's eye or foot becomes struck off, one is to pay
up the whole value to him
— [*88* **81**]   If someone binds someone's handyman, he is to compensate
6 sh.

[IX COMPENSATION FOR SLAVES]
— [*89* **82**]   Slave's highway-robbery is to be 3 shillings
— [*90* **83**]   If a slave steals, one is to compensate with payment x 2

3. Explanatory Comments

The first thing likely to occur to modern readers of these laws is that they
are very unlike anything we would expect to find in a parliamentary statute
or local by-law today. All the same, we do not need to spend long mulling
over these staccato clauses to find that they are actually about many of the
things that concern contemporary law: the status of government agencies,
compensation for death or injury, security of property (especially
boundaries), sexual aggression and women's rights. The differences from
our approach to these subjects lie in the way that Æthelberht's laws are
formulated, and the sort of sanctions and remedies they offer. The
following comments address (a) their style of formulation, (b) their
approach to righting of wrongs, then (c) the particular reasons why
Æthelberht may have issued them, and (d), last but far from least, the fact
that they were written in English: they are not only the earliest surviving
English document but by also by far the earliest text of any kind in
something like the language we still use.

(a) *Style*

The text's most obvious feature is its artless simplicity of expression. The
great majority of clauses consist of 'If' followed by a particular
contingency, then pronouncement of stipulated consequences. As against
that dominant pattern, just three clauses in a total of 127 begin with a
relative clause ('He who…': 22:1, 47, 51), and thirty-two, half of these

evidently 'sub-sections', address topics directly ('For…': 1-7, 14, 16:2, 17, 20, 21:1-2, 22:2, 27:2, 48-48:3, 59-60:1, 67:2-3, 70:1. 71:1, 73-74:3, 82); only one clause is linked to its predecessor by a conjunction ('And…': 60:1). This style of legislation can be found in the Twelve Tables, the foundation document of Roman Law, and the Law of Moses (though not the Ten Commandments). Anyone familiar with a will or a tax-return will know that one of the things about written law is that it veers towards the (over-)complex. This is because a wholly written legal system simply has to cover all possible eventualities. In orally conditioned systems, alternative possibilities can be left to the skills (or common-sense) of the parties and their representatives. The message of Æthelberht's simple syntax, and it is simpler than other codes of about this time [*see below 3(c) Making Written Law*] is thus that the text is exceptionally close to the sort of law which, before the advent of writing, would have been kept in the heads of the more experienced citizens. One other point, though the details are too technical to discuss here, is that the grammar of the 'Personal Injury' section is yet more archaic than that of the rest of the text, implying that this part in particular is even likelier to have been memorized by experts.

(b) *Righting Wrongs*

The salient characteristic of these laws is that, almost without exception they demand that sums of money, 'shillings' and their sub-species, *scætta*, be paid by the offender to the offended party, whether God (1), king (8-17), or 'bride's father' (76:1). (Early money is a complex topic, too: all that needs saying here is that 'shillings' and *scætta* were <u>weights</u> of gold or silver which might take the form of a coin, of other precious objects, or of metal weights like those used on scales in pre-electronic days.) To understand the prominence of payment, we must go a long way beyond early English law and consider the place of 'feud', revenge, in the world's less developed legal systems. Perceptions of early English law were transformed half a century ago by social anthropologists (a classic essay, by Max Gluckman, is in *Further Reading*). What they showed is that, contrary to what we might expect, feud is a *source of peace*.

We may start with a story in the great early English epic poem, *Beowulf*, always a good idea in thinking about early English history [*see below 4(a)*]. The hero, Beowulf himself, is briefing his king about the politics of Denmark, from where he has recently returned after fighting off the monsters plaguing the royal hall. He prophesies that the Danish king's strategy for pacifying the feud of Dane and 'Heathobard' will not work. That king's idea was that his daughter would be a 'peace-weaver' between his people and their traditional Heathobard enemies by marrying the heir to the Heathobard throne.   However, a drunken retainer will not be able to abide seeing his father's sword flaunted by his killer's son; 'After the death of a prince', comments the hero sagely, 'it is rare for the spear to lie idle for long, however beautiful the bride'.   Fighting will therefore burst out anew at the very wedding reception, doubtless fuelled by copious intake of wine, beer and mead. The hall that Beowulf had ridded of its alien visitors will itself, we have already been told, be burned down as a consequence.

This story is strikingly echoed in Bede's *Ecclesiastical History* [*see below 4(b)*].   In a battle between the Northumbrians and the Mercians (679), a prisoner of war who had pretended to be a rustic not a nobleman (i.e. a fighter) was betrayed by his 'appearance, bearing and speech', revealing that he was really a nobleman (with an 'upper-class accent').   His captor declares that, as such, he is liable to vengeance for 'all my brothers and kinsmen - killed in the battle'. However, he decided to sell him as a slave instead; only, his chains kept falling off because his brother, thinking him dead, was praying for his soul, so that he was finally able to return to tell the tale.   In the chapter introducing the story, Bede says the Northumbrian king's brother was killed in the battle too, which was 'good reason for sharper fighting and more prolonged enmity between these kings and fierce peoples'. Happily, Archbishop Theodore was able to make peace, by ensuring that 'a due sum of money' was paid to the vengeful king. Here, then, the ceaseless cycle of revenge to which a killing might have given rise is assuaged by payment of money. This is the sort of monetary payment we find in Æthelberht 's code, and others like it: 'due sums of money', which *put an end to feud.*

The first point to grasp about the feuding process in this sort of society is that revenge was as much social duty as emotional compulsion.   This was undoubtedly one of the main sources of violence in a violent society. But compensation might also be offered as a substitute for the satisfaction to be had by taking revenge.   Among the Kamba of colonial Kenya, seven bulls and a cow might be paid for a life, while a goat could cover loss of a tooth. Similarly, the Roman historian, Tacitus, tells us that among the early Germanic peoples from whom the new masters of Kent derived, culprits paid over a number of horses and cattle, 'part going to the king or tribe, and part to the injured man or his relatives'.   So anti-social activity was discouraged by knowing that the other could only be prevented from taking it out on you physically by coming up with a large sum of money; and injured parties would be encouraged to accept payment proportionate to their loss by knowing that if they resorted to violence, the other side could then do so too, resulting in interminable tit-for-tat killing.   The second point is that not only perpetrators but also their whole family, at least as far as second cousins, were exposed to their victim's vengeance, so just as liable to buy it off as the offender personally.   If a Smith kills a Jones, *any* Jones can kill *any* Smith.   In the circumstances, the Smiths as a whole would have every incentive to help their erring relative to find the money.   Womenfolk like the Danish king's daughter, sprung from one family and married into the other, would have a particular motive to urge restraint.   In fact, all of a family's easier-going members would be anxious to control the aggressive impulses of their hotheads, so functioning as policemen too.   In feuding society, therefore, the prospect of revenge is both the deterrent to wrong, and the main reason to settle 'out of court'. Before dismissing this sort of legal system out of hand, we should perhaps reflect that a constant complaint about our modern legal system is that it takes inadequate account of the feelings or interests of victims.

This, then, is why Æthelberht's laws are so preoccupied with money payments.   They are called '*leodgeld*', 'person payment' (13, 24, 64), or '*wergeld*', 'man payment' (31), i.e. 'blood-money'. The commonest words in the text after 'if' are '*bot*, compensation', and the verb deriving from it, '*gebetan*'. We can see too that the amount of compensation due was determined by the sufferer's status. A king himself was entitled to all of fifty shillings for infringement of his 'protection', and ninefold restitution for loss of his property (8, 10-12, 14, 16). A noble ('earl') got twelve shillings (18-19), a commoner ('*ceorl*') six (20-20:1, 22, 23-23:1, 26, 28). For killing *ceorls* one paid 100 shillings, twice the royal protection (24); killing an earl was apparently at this stage inconceivable: we only know from the next Kentish code [*see below 4(d)*] that the sum due was 300 shillings, three times what was payable for a *ceorl* (by then, in West Saxon law, the multiplier was six). In short, some people's blood was more valuable than others'. All conceivable parts of one's body had their specific value (33-71:1). The integrity of one's home ('enclosure') and marriage was upheld on the same basis as life and limb (27-32). The rights of women were not ignored but were understood largely in terms of their value to their male relatives: royal widows were worth fifty shillings to their protector (74, compare other ranks, 74:1-3); a widow might retain a life interest in her husband's goods, even if she remarried, but only if she had borne children; otherwise she must surrender even the sum compensating her for her virginal bloodshed the morning after (76:2-5); men are entitled to their money back if they turn out to have invested in unsatisfactory goods (76-76:1).

One other thing should be noted. In clause 15 a free man who steals from another is punished not only by paying the loser three times the value of the stolen goods but also a 'fine for that' to the king and if unable to raise the money must apparently surrender to him his entire property. Similarly, the victim of an assault or her family receives 35 shillings. but the king gets 15 shillings as well (77:2). It was in this direction that English law would be going by the later seventh century when we next have codes. Kings are far more often recipients of what we may now call fines than in Æthelberht's time; and they more frequently demand that deviants be flogged, sold as slaves, even executed. By the tenth century, royal action is the norm, and *bot* is payable not to victims and/or their families but to the king, or God (i.e. the Church).   We may by that stage, if not under Æthelberht, think in terms of 'Crime' and 'Punishment'.

(c)   *Making Written Law*

To our modern eye, it seems obvious that it is better to put law in writing than to leave it in the fallible memory of even the most trusted judge. That cannot be how it would have looked to Æthelberht's contemporaries. For we may, and in the light of anthropological researches we actually should, assume that law and order were quite well preserved among Kentish people long before it was committed to parchment.   What, then, was in it for the king?   Why did he and his councillors feel a need to make a statement like this?   If the motive were simply to 'reform' the law, for instance by introducing, or perhaps raising, the payments due for insult and injury, then resorting to the unfamiliar medium of script would not be the most obvious way to set about it.   In any case, payment, even increased payment, would have been the norm in a preliterate system; and we have already seen that the style of the code makes it look like traditional law hitherto preserved in the authorities' heads. We need to understand not only that customary law is almost by definition unwritten, but at the same time that not all unwritten law is merely traditional. Preliterate cultures must have been able not only to preserve and enforce their law by word of mouth but also to change it.   A partial parallel is the Laws of Cricket.   These have of course been in writing since the early nineteenth century, but the game had very largely evolved by then; they are still changed by MCC statute — members might think almost annually — but players of the game do not need to mull over the pavilion copy before marching out to face a new LBW rule; and even umpires are as likely to learn about innovations from colleagues as from their own text.

The first clue as to what Æthelberht was up to comes from Bede [*see below 4(c)*].   First, these laws were 'conferred on his people…with the counsel of his wise men'.   Like most law-makers, Æthelberht acted only with 'advice and consent'.   His wise men were not elected and were representative only in so far as they were the kingdom's more eminent and experienced (and so, usually, older) subjects; even today, statutes are made by 'Queen in Parliament', and life-peers (or whatever replace them) are likely to have been qualified for their role by their experience. Secondly, Bede calls them 'enacted judgments (*decreta iudiciorum*)'. That is my translation of a difficult phrase. But *'decreta'* should have its literal meaning of what is 'decreed', presumably in writing; while *'iudicium'*, literally 'judgment', seems likely to correspond to the Old English word *'dom'*, with the same meaning. The old-fashioned may still say that they 'deem' something, that is, 'judge'; our word 'law' was one of the less baleful legacies of the Viking invasions! We find this word *'dom'* in the prologues of the next two Kentish codes [*see below 4(d)*]: Hlothere and Eadric 'pronounce these judgments (*thissum domum*)', Wihtræd lays down 'these decrees (*thas domas*)'. Yet note too that these kings are 'increasing' or 'adding to' law; furthermore, Hlothere and Eadric envisage that the law they are supplementing was 'produced before' by 'their elders'. In other words, what elders like Æthelberht and his council had issued had by then become 'established law', indeed 'custom '[*see below 4(e)*]. By virtue of 'finding' judgments, they created a law that itself became traditional, as was, as Bede says, 'held and observed - to this day'.

This may account for Bede's use of one particular phrase, but does not explain why Kent's rulers decided to make their laws in writing. To understand this, we must turn to Bede's next phrase, 'following the examples of the Romans'. The Roman Empire was then, indirectly, and for much of the world still is, the pre-eminent law-making power. When 'barbarian' (i.e. Germanic-speaking) kings took over its government after the fifth century, most proceeded to issue codes of written law. Æthelberht's in-laws, the kings of the Franks, for example, had produced the 'Salic Law', *Lex Salica*, which speciously dictated the succession of male kings down to the French Revolution. It is possible to show that the very structure of Æthelberht's code (Church - king - noble - freeman - injury - women) may have followed a model probably issued by a council at Paris in 614, chaired by Æthelberht's cousin-by-marriage — and attended by the Bishop of Rochester and by the Abbot of St Augustine's (who drowned in the Channel on the way home). Its list of injuries compares closely with that in codes issued about or after this date; it is as if a people's 'injury tariff' was a mark of its legal identity, so carefully memorized by those aspiring to a judicial or law-giving role. At the same time, Rome had come to stand for Catholic orthodoxy too: it was a Pope who prompted Æthelberht's conversion. To repeat, Christianity was the vehicle of literacy to post-Roman culture. In 'following the examples of the Romans', therefore, the king of Kent was entering the civilized world where Christian kings lived up to imperial and biblical standards, not to mention their neighbours', by making written law, however otherwise irrelevantly. To have law in writing did not make it any easier to change or enforce, but did, simply, make it look better. That is not quite the end of it, however. It is an important point that Æthelberht's code as it stands was *not* issued in his name. Our only good evidence of his responsibility for it is Bede's passage. This, once again, was the pattern of Frankish legislation. Neither the first Christian king of the Franks, Clovis (486-511) nor Charlemagne himself (768-814) put their name at the head of *Lex Salica,* whose preface is chiefly a hymn to the greatness of the Franks as a people. In the first instance, it was the *Cantwara,* not their king, who came out of the code looking civilized.

Yet by the late-seventh century, law *was* officially the business of Kings Hlothere, Eadric, Wihtræd, Ine, the last even supposing that it would boost his 'kingship'. Further, we have already seen that the laws of Æthelberht's successors in Kent and of their West Saxon counterpart were much more aggressive than he was about their role in punishment and entitlement to the proceeds. What this suggests is that merely by enhancing their law-making persona, by joining the family of 'civilized' nations, kings were moving towards a position where they both dictated and profited from the law. In making 'established law' and 'custom' by pronouncing 'judgment', they put themselves in a position where they could expect to receive more fines, more confiscated property (15). To this extent, Æthelberht's code is a first step in the prolonged evolution of English criminal jurisprudence.

(d) *English Speech*

One other feature of Æthelberht's text and of Bede's account of it is of the utmost importance: that it was 'written in English speech (*Anglicum sermone*)'. Because Roman emperors naturally made law in Latin, so too did their originally Germanic-speaking successors. Even when legislating for their territory across the Rhine, where Latin had never been spoken, Frankish kings issued Latin codes, though larded with Germanic technical terms. Æthelberht's code was therefore unique: only Celtic and (later) Scandinavian lands had vernacular laws. It is not at first obvious why this should be so. If the use of Latin was itself part of 'the examples of the Romans', why did Æthelberht not 'follow' it that far? One answer, that there were not people able to put English law in Latin, only takes us so far; we still need to explain why Æthelberht's new bishops were less able to grapple with Germanic technicalities than whoever it was that enabled Frankish kings to issue *Lex Salica* in Latin. One other possibility is therefore worth a moment's thought. The chief reason why written Old English made far greater strides through the centuries until the Norman Conquest than any continental vernacular is probably that so many Englishmen were converted by Irish missionaries, who used their own language habitually at home; but it may be significant too that Theodore (669-90), 'the first archbishop whom the whole English Church obeyed', in Bede's telling phrase, was a Greek (in fact he was from St Paul's home town of Tarsus). Self-confident Greek culture was always more tolerant of non-classical languages than the aggressively insecure Latins: Greek speakers gave Goths and later Slavs their own vernacular Scriptures. So it *may* be significant too that Gregory had himself been papal legate in Constantinople before his elevation to St Peter's chair. Even if he knew no Greek himself (as he insisted, unconvincingly), he might have seen at first-hand what the Church could gain by fostering the language of its converts. His missionaries could have been similarly broad-minded.

However this may be, the 'English speech' of Æthelberht's code was hardly less important in its long-term consequences than his adoption of a central role in law-making. Almost all legislation from then until 1066 was in Old English. and only translated into Latin by Francophones in the twelfth century.   By the last century of the Old English kingdom 'writs', orders sent by the king to shire courts were in English too. For over three centuries thereafter, law was made and applied in Latin or French.   But the gentry who ran shire government under their sheriff must still have spoken English at home.   The proof is that from the later fourteenth century, English staged a remarkable 'come-back', first as the Literature of Chaucer, and before long as law made by Council and Parliament.   In other words, there is an at least indirect connection between the fact that England is today the world's oldest continuously functioning state and that English is its most widely spoken language.   England's language and law are the most enduring marks of Englishness, its main claims to anyone else's attention.   The history of both begins with Æthelberht.   I can think of no better reason to erect a statue of him and his Frankish queen.   In fact, I am rather appalled that it was not done long ago.

4.   Relevant Evidence

(a) *Beowulf lines 2024 - 64*

Freawaru ... was promised to Prince Ingeld of the Heathobards: [her father] reckons it a good idea to settle the series of murderous feuds [between Danes and Heathobards].   But after the death of a prince it is rare for the spear to remain idle for long, however good the bride! For it may disturb the prince of the Heathobards, and every thegn of his people, when he enters the hall with his woman, that the treasures of the Heathobards, the arms and armour that their ancestors once wielded, should glitter on the backs of [the] Danes.   Sooner or later, when the drinking has begun, some fierce old spearman who remembers the massacre of his comrades will recognize one of the swords.   He will begin to stir up some young fellow ...until one of the woman's thegns, lying soaked in blood from a sword-cut, loses his life for his father's deeds (*fore fæder daedum*). Then on both sides the sworn word of nobles will be broken...

(b) *Bede's Eccl. Hist.* iv 21-2

A great battle was fought [between Northumbrians and Mercians] ... and the king's brother was killed ... Although there was good reason for sharper fighting and more prolonged enmity between the kings and fierce peoples, Archbishop Theodore completely extinguished the outbreak of so great and dangerous a fire ... The kings and peoples on either side were pacified, no one's life was given for slaying the king's brother, but merely a due sum of money (*debita multa ... pecuniae*) to the avenging king ... In this battle ... among the casualties was a young man [among] the soldiery called Imma.   After lying like the dead among the corpses of the slain for that day and the following night, he recovered consciousness and, reviving, bandaged his wounds as best he could ... ... But ... he was captured by men of the enemy army and taken to their lord ... Asked who he was, he was afraid to admit that he was a soldier (*militem*): rather, he replied that he was a countryman (*rusticum*) and poor and married ... ... His captor took care of his wounds, and when he began to get better ordered that he be bound at night lest he escape ... ... When he had been held for some time, those who watched him realized from his appearance, clothing and speech that he was not a commoner ... but a noble. [His captor] promised that he would do him no harm if he would simply reveal who he was. When he revealed that he was a servant of the king, he replied, "Now you deserve to die because all my brothers and relatives were killed in that battle; but I shall not kill you, lest I break my promise' ... ...So, when Imma got better, he sold him to a Frisian in London ...

(c) *Bede's Eccl. Hist.* ii 5

Among the other benefits which he thoughtfully conferred on his people, he also established enacted judgments for them, following the examples of the Romans (*decreta illi iudiciorum iuxta exempla Romanorum*), with the counsel of his wise men. These were written in English speech, and are held and observed by them to this day ...

(d) *Laws of Hlothere and Eadric (?679-86).*

Hlothere and Eadric, kings of the Kent-people, increased the law (*ecton þa ae*) that their elders produced before with these judgments (*ðyssum domum*) that are pronounced hereafter.

(e) *Laws of Wihtræd (September 6th 695) - at Bearsted.*

There the powerful with the consent of all laid down these decrees (*das domas*) and added to the just customs of the Kent-people (*Cantwara rihtum peawum*) as it hereafter says and declares: ... .

5. Further Reading

F.L. Attenborough, *The Laws of the Earliest English Kings* (Cambridge, 1922), pp. 4-17: the version in use until recently (by Richard's and David's father).

L. Oliver, *The Beginnings of English Law* (Toronto, 2002), pp. 60-81:   in every way a huge improvement; perhaps significantly by an American.

D. Whitelock, *English Historical Documents, vol. I, c. 550-1042* (London, 2nd edn, 1979), pp. 391-4.
Should be in public library.   Magisterial translation but omitting many clauses, including 'injury tariff'.

F. Liebermann, *Die Gesetze der Angelsachsen* (3 vols, Halle, 1903-16) vol I, pp. 3-8.
Definitive scholarly edition, by a German-Jewish scholar who lost his English friends when he spoke up for German war-claims in the dedication of his third volume.

P.H. Sawyer, *Textus Roffensis* (Early English Manuscripts in Facsimile VII, Copenhagen, 1957), fols. lr-4r. Those wanting to see what the code looks like on the page may also find this in a public or cathedral library.

P.H. Sawyer, *From Roman Britain to Norman England* (London, 2nd edn, 1998), pp. 172-3, 188-90: perhaps the best short account of Æthelberht's laws.

P. Wormald, *The Making of English Law. vol I. Legislation and its Limits* (Oxford, 1999), pp. 93-101: full discussion, but probably only manageable by specialists!

All these editions and discussions cover the laws of Æthelberht's Kentish successors.

M. Gluckman, '*The Peace in the Feud*', ch. 1 of Gluckman, *Custom and Conflict in Africa* (Oxford, 1956): the essay that changed how historians think about this sort of law.